Wealth Path

Get On It!

The Only Wealth Building Book You Need

J.D. Church

2009

The best way to order copies of this book is at: https://www.createspace.com/3388769

You can also go to www.amazon.com and search for Wealth Path in the books category.

If you would like a recommendation on where to get additional financial and business education information for yourself, your spouse, your children, your relatives, your friends, and the many other people you know who could benefit from this kind of financial and business literacy after you have read this book send an email to: contact@wealthpathbook.com with the subject line: "I Must Get Financially Educated".

If you'd like to arrange for a speaking engagement with the author at one of your events or in your classroom send an email to: contact@wealthpathbook.com with the subject line: "Speaking Event".

If you'd like to arrange a book signing event with the author send an email to: contact@wealthpathbook.com with the subject line: "Book Signing".

Contents

Dedication

This book is dedicated to people everywhere, at any age and education level, who want to escape, or never enter, the debt driven life-style. May you avoid becoming a "Broke-A-Holic" by learning and applying the 2 Steps to Wealth outlined in this book.

Disclaimer

This book, as with any book on personal or business financial management and planning, is written as a general guide. No guarantee, express or implied, is made that by reading this book an individual, business, or other entity will become rich or wealthy as each individual and business situation is unique and requires specific planning considerations and strategies based on those unique and ever changing situations.

All persons reading this book and applying its principles should consult with a certified financial planner and a licensed tax advisor when outlining or executing specific financial and tax planning strategies for their personal or business use.

<u>Quotes</u>

Personal goal setting is the strongest force in the world. −Paul J. Meyer

Personal goal getting is the most rewarding force in the world. Set your goals and surpass them! −Jeff Church

You can't change your past but you can change your future by doing what you always do routinely, differently today. −Jeff Church

Introduction

This is the only "how to get rich or wealthy" book you will ever need to read if you apply its two steps.

The simplicity of this book is amazing. The depth of its perceptions and your understanding and application of them can be profound. You should gain new insights with every reading.

Many books have been written, read, and studied on this topic. This book eliminates the fluff and provides you the executive summary of how to become rich or wealthy starting with decisions you can make right now.

The sooner you start applying the principles outlined in this book the sooner you will begin or speed up your journey towards financial literacy and becoming rich or wealthy.

This book is ideal for high school freshmen through graduates, college freshmen through graduates, people pursuing or having graduate degrees, and anyone else who will need to utilize money during their life.

The book is for anyone, at any age, anywhere. It does focus in chapter 4 on business and financial matters as they apply in the United States. However, anyone reading the book outside of the United States can still learn and apply the principles discussed as they pertain to each reader's specific country.

All of the chapters contain powerful wealth information for everyone to read, understand, and apply. The book moves progressively to more complex, yet very important, rich and wealth building content between chapters 1 and 4. Chapter 4 contains a lot of information that is critical to building first riches, then wealth, and then for sustaining and passing on that wealth. All of this starts with the 2 Steps discussed in Chapter 1 and the 75/25 = 3 formula discussed in Chapter 2.

Chapter 3 contains information about why most people never become rich or wealthy by any definition. Although many of the items talked about in this chapter seem to be minor individually, collectively they either lead you down the Wealth Path or they rob you of your wealth potential every day. These conditions exist for good or bad because of choices and decisions you make and the things you do or do not do. Change your daily choices and your daily actions and you will change your financial future.

Do not skip over chapter 4, especially the Self-Directed Retirement Plan (SDRP) portion, because you "don't understand it". What this book covers in chapter 4 are key components to becoming rich and wealthy. Learn what each of those SDRP bullets means and use that information. You can use all the information in chapter 4 from the day you are born up until the day you die. You can use it for any size and any kind of legitimate business as well. If you've done it right, what you set up will continue even after you do die.

It is never too early or too late to set up your estate plan. Although this book only briefly mentions estate planning in chapter 4, this is an extremely important part of wealth and should start as early in life as possible. Estate planning is not something you wait until you become rich or wealthy to do; it is something you do and then revise as you progress through the different stages of rich and wealthy.

Several times in this book I invite you to "Get Financially and Business Educated" by sending an email to contact@wealthpathbook.com with a subject line: "I Must Get Financially Educated". There is much to understand about becoming rich or wealthy and no one person or book is the "expert" in all things. Doing what is in this book will get you on the Wealth Path but what you should realize after reading it is that you need a team of experts, on many different subjects, that vary depending on where you are on the Wealth Path, who, under your informed and educated direction, assist in putting together your plan for becoming rich or wealthy. Once started you and they then maintain and grow that plan for the remainder of your life and as long after your life as you desire. You never stop getting more financial and business education once you commit to becoming rich or wealthy. That learning process is a lifelong endeavor.

Once I got on the Wealth Path through my financial literacy and business education, team of experts, books I read, and seminars I attend, the net worth of my business and assets that I controlled increased from right around $100,000 (alive) to just over $1 million. Much of that was in real estate even though many are now saying real estate is a "terrible investment." In 2007 I controlled, through my business, one real estate deal that was by itself, valued at nearly $3 million, with literally no money down and that's during this "bad market." In 2008 I helped, at no charge, a married soldier who was on his way back to Kuwait and Iraq for a second tour, get his house out of foreclosure. That is a great feeling to be able to help a family like that. In my business, now that I am becoming financially and business educated every day, I can help people. Don't everyone email or call me now asking for the same foreclosure help. His situation was unique and I am not a non-profit charity. If you really want my help, help yourself by reading this book, the books I suggest and others, and by asking me how I did it and then by taking your own action.

Real estate is never a terrible investment when you are educated in how to find, assess, acquire control, and have an exit strategy already planned. Real estate, whether the market is up, down, or level is a valuable wealth building tool when you know how to do more than just offer $10,000 less than the asking price and settle on "splitting the difference." Real estate is and will continue to be where the wealthy make, shelter, and grow their riches and wealth. I will continue to use real estate and its associated fields to find opportunities to grow wealth. I also now have the opportunity to grow wealth while helping others learn the 2 Steps to riches or wealth and about becoming financially and business literate from speaking engagements, book signings, and book sales.

People have said and will continue to say that I was lucky, or it worked for me but not for them, or I'm a lot smarter than they are because they could never understand all that information, or they are too old or too young, or they have no time, and every other excuse in the book to justify to themselves why I could do it but they could not. Guess what, me too. Get over it and get started. The sooner the better. The conditions for you to get started will never be right. You will never have enough money, time, or be the right age. That's why you have to get educated now and start now. Reading this book is a good start or reminder.

When those same people ask how I got started in my business and I tell them they are amazed that I spent over $50,000 to get educated and start my real estate business. They say they don't have that kind of money to start a business. Guess what, neither did I. Was it worth it for me to spend $50,000 for a financial and business education in addition to my traditional bachelor's and master's degrees? Of course it was. Guess what, you can do it and you don't have to spend $50,000 doing it. I will tell you exactly how I did it and how you can do it for less. Will it cost something? Of course, even if it is just your time. Will it be worth it? Of course it will if you decide to take action. Even if I go bust tomorrow I will still have the knowledge of how to start a business, maximize tax and legal strategies, and generate passive income again. Do I still have a day job? Of course, because I'm a recovering "Broke-A-Holic" and don't meet this book's definition of wealthy – yet!

At the end of this book, in addition to my offer for you to "Get Financially and Business Educated," there is a short list of other books you may want to read in addition to the IRS publications I mention in chapter 4. There are many other books out there that you should read about business, finances, real estate, stocks, taxes, estate planning and the like. My recommended list is just to get you started or to remind you what you should be doing. I tell you now though that simply reading and knowing will not get you on the Wealth Path without some "doing" on your part. Doing is what makes the difference.

When you accept my invitation to get additional financial and business literacy education I will refer you to the team of "experts" I have learned from and worked with.

Be forewarned, they are not a charity group. They are professionals in their fields and as with obtaining any education and services there is cost associated with that knowledge and their services. Fortunately, after reading this book you will realize that the question is not, "How much does it cost?" but rather, "How much can you make?" by getting financially and business educated and by getting a team of "experts" together to assist you every step of the way as you need it.

There is also a section in this book titled, "Your Actions." The intent of these pages is for you to write down things that will assist you in getting on the Wealth Path. If you write in this section of the book I suggest you do so using pencil. I have found, over the years, that even my best plans seem to change and it is much easier to erase pencil and make necessary modifications than it is to erase pen. However, if you are like me you would almost never actually write in a book so have some paper or note cards handy as you read so that you can jot down your actions as you think of them. Don't tell yourself that you'll write them down when you're done reading because by the time you're done reading you will have forgotten a lot of what came to mind earlier. Before getting into the rest of the book, go get paper and pencil ready so you can make your Action notes as you think of them.

From this point forward your financial future can change forever. Are You Ready?

The 2 Steps

Step 1: To Be Rich. Live on 75% of what you earn and save the difference in compounding, interest bearing accounts, consistently, over time.

Step 2: To Be Wealthy. Live on 75% of what you earn and invest the difference in ever increasing income producing assets.

Those are the two steps. Once you understand and apply them in your life, or in the life of your business, you can become rich or wealthy. The choice of which is yours.

You could stop reading now. That's it.

If you're interested in ideas on how to apply these two steps keep reading but first we need to define rich and wealthy.

For this book rich means you have enough money left over every month, after paying all your expenses, to live a life you consider comfortable. Expenses include food, shelter, taxes, medical, dental, insurance, transportation, communication, and clothing. Rich means if you stopped working you would no longer have enough income to cover your monthly expenses after six months. Obviously, the amount of money you need to consider yourself rich will differ from the amount others will need to consider themselves rich because it depends completely on your opinion of a rich life. Rich in this book, at any income level, means you have to keep working to keep money coming into your pocket to cover all of your expenses and still have some money left over.

For this book wealthy means you have enough money left over every month, after paying all your expenses, to live a life you consider comfortable without ever having to work to earn money again. You could lie in bed all month, doing nothing, and you would still have that money coming into your pocket. To be wealthy in this book, you have to have your money and assets working and making money for you 24/7/365 and have enough passive income to pay all your expenses and live what you consider to be a wealthy life. Wealthy in this book, at any income level, means you do not have to work to keep enough money coming into your pocket to cover all of your expenses and have some left over. Whether you decide to work or not, how much to work, or how long to work, is completely up to you. There is nothing wrong with working even when you are wealthy and don't really have to work.

Decide now if you will be rich or wealthy because the rest of this book is about getting there.

The 2 Steps Defined

75/25 = 3. This is the only formula you need to remember and apply. It can make you rich or wealthy. What does this formula mean? 75 represents living on 75% of your income. 25 represents using 25% for charitable giving and investing in income producing assets.   3 represents the 3 points listed below. 75/25 = 3 is a flexible formula as you will learn in this book.

1. Live on 75% of what you earn. It does not matter if you get paid daily, weekly, bi-monthly, monthly, quarterly, or annually or what level of income you have from your job or business. If you only use 75% of what you earn for living you can become rich by saving the difference in compounding, interest bearing accounts, consistently, over time. If you only use 75% of what you earn for living you can become wealthy by investing the difference in ever increasing income producing assets. Stop keeping up with other people or businesses and showing off your money by living at or beyond your means and start taking care of your own long-term financial well-being. The sooner you begin, the sooner you will start becoming rich or wealthy. Staying out of

bad debt and collecting interest instead of paying interest should lead to a better financial life for you.

2. Donate 10% of what you earn to a charitable organization. Giving to those who need and to causes that help will bring you a sense of well-being and accomplishment as well as provide you legitimate tax benefits. This should help you live a better life overall. This should help you understand you have an abundant life right now compared to those you help.

3. Invest 15% of what you earn in compounding, interest bearing accounts to become rich or in acquiring and growing income producing assets to become wealthy.

For our less experienced audience let's briefly mention some compounding, interest bearing accounts and then some income producing assets. First the compounding, interest bearing accounts could be savings accounts, checking accounts, money market accounts, certificates of deposit, and loans you make to others that you charge an interest rate on. Some income producing assets could be owning your own business, owning investment real estate such as rental units, royalties on books, movies, television shows, and music you make, patents you own and sell rights to, stocks and mutual fund dividends, and more.

Don't confuse an asset with a liability. An asset is something that puts money into your pocket. A liability is something that takes money out of your pocket. You can have good expenses or debts that put more money in your pocket than they take out. Those good expenses or debts are assets not liabilities. Keep and grow them. Assets can become liabilities. Liabilities can become assets.

It's simple: Assets = Money In Your Pocket. Liabilities = Money Out of Your Pocket. There are no exceptions or justifications. It is black or white, right or wrong, good or bad, when determining if something is an asset or liability. There are some liabilities that are worth having and keeping. Don't invest in a liability and call it an asset. Follow the money and you will know which it really is.

The 75/25 = 3 formula is not a law for riches or wealth. It is flexible. If you can live on 50% of what you earn, donate 10%, and use 40% to acquire and grow assets this could increase the rate at which you become rich and wealthy. If you must, live on 90% of what you earn, donate 5%, and use 5% to acquire and grow assets. This could slow the rate at which you become rich and wealthy.

The rich law is that you must live on less than you earn and save the difference in compounding, interest bearing accounts, consistently, over time. This is not flexible.

The wealthy law is you must live on less than you earn and invest the difference in ever increasing income producing assets. This is not flexible.

These two laws apply to personal and business finances regardless of the type or size of personal or business finances. Break these laws and you will not be rich, wealthy, or in a profitable business.

You can change your financial future right now just by deciding to apply these two simple laws and this one simple formula, 75/25 = 3, to your personal and business life. Of course, after you decide to do it you will have to actually do it. It doesn't work if you only think about it. You think and grow rich by taking action. You live the law of attraction by taking action. You prepare and you act.

Do it! Change the future by changing your financial future!

Y U R a Broke-A-Holic

For most of you reading this book you are broke because you choose to be broke nearly every day of your life. You choose to live on more than you earn. You choose to spend all that you earn or more. You choose not to invest in assets that bring more money in. You confuse needs and wants. You do not make maximum use of tax laws to benefit yourself financially. You don't have your own business. You are not willing to wait until you have cash on hand to make purchases so you buy on ever increasing credit card debt. You do not track all of your income and all of your expenditures. You are broke because you don't know any other way than being in debt. You believe the advertising that tells you that you deserve everything, right now, and that you can get it all for a low, monthly payment.

Listed later in this chapter are some considerations to think about and choices you can make to stop being broke and have money to invest in compounding, interest bearing accounts or income producing assets.

In addition to better managing the income you do have, get yourself financially educated. Become financially literate. If you do not understand how money works, how interest works, how assets work, and how to protect your assets you will not become rich or wealthy. If you do become rich or wealthy through some lucky chance you will not keep that money if you are not financially literate. The time to become financially literate is now, before you have more riches or wealth to lose.

Get yourself a legitimate small business started and running. Get a financial advisor or an accountant to help you. Get credit counseling so you understand and maximize credit policies that help you raise your credit score. Read books about financial management. Make and stick to a budget (call this a Wealth Plan) by first tracking every penny of income and every penny of expense. Know where all your money comes from and where all of your money is going. Once you know how your money flows you will be able to identify the places you need to and can make adjustments. This is equally as true for your personal finances as it is for your business finances.

Budgeting does not mean you stop spending money. Budgeting does not mean you have no fun and skimp on everything. Budgeting _does_ mean you have a written financial Wealth Plan for becoming rich or wealthy by living on less than you earn and investing the difference in assets. Budgeting _does_ mean you have a written plan for having fun without racking up more and more credit card debt that you pay 18% or 21% interest on every month.

Your fun will be even more fun when you don't have delayed debt with interest hanging over your head for the next 15 years. Budgeting, using a Wealth Plan, is one way to increase your wealth and fun. Budgeting is a goal. Set your budgeting goal and then surpass your goal. If you don't write down your budgeting goals you will most likely never achieve them. Build in fun and rewards for yourself and your business when you achieve your budgeting goals. Make getting rich and wealthy fun.

Imagine the time when interest will work in your favor. Imagine how much sooner you will become rich or wealthy when instead of paying 18% interest you are receiving 18% interest every month. Interest and time are excellent ways to begin to become rich, and later, wealthy. If every 12 year old will put $25 into a compounding, 8% interest bearing account every month until they turn 65 years old they should live an enjoyable retirement. If every 20 year old will put $100 into a compounding, 8% interest bearing account every month they should live an enjoyable retirement. Not just from this money, but from the other good financial habits they will have developed and lived during their walk on the Wealth Path.

Interest is either good or bad for you. Most people are broke because they never collect on the financial benefits of compounding interest over time. The sooner you start paying yourself this monthly investment the more money you will acquire in the long run. Start saving today. This is investing in your best asset; yourself.

Let's face it. You are carrying debt. Some of you carry a little; some of you carry a lot. Stop carrying unnecessary debt and paying that interest that just keeps you living the life of a "Broke-A-Holic". Easy to say but how do you get out from under this debt? Play the slots and buy lottery tickets and hope to win big of course. NO! Make a Wealth Plan. Track all of your income and all of your expenses. Pay yourself first, every time you get paid or have money come in. Living 75/25 = 3 is the way.

Start paying yourself first by getting rid of your interest bearing debts. When you make your Wealth Plan you will know all of your debts. One way is to identify the interest bearing debt with the lowest pay-off balance. All your other interest bearing debts make the minimum payments on. Don't skip or pay less than you owe as this could damage your credit rating. Pay the minimum payments on all but that one debt with the lowest pay-off amount. For that one debt, pay as much as possible, every month, until the debt is eliminated. Then roll that total amount you were paying onto the next debt with the lowest payoff. Add the first payment to the minimum payment you were making. Use this "domino effect" to pay off those debts that are keeping you broke by charging you compounding interest over time. Once your debts are paid off take all of that money and start investing in compounding, interest bearing accounts or income producing assets.

One key to success with this plan is to not go back and charge up those interest bearing accounts after you pay them off. There is nothing wrong with using the accounts, just do not let them accumulate that huge amount of interest bearing debt on them again. You must live on less than you earn even after you pay off debts if you are going to have money to invest towards becoming rich or wealthy.

If you can't make the minimum payments on your debt, contact the creditor and see if you can rearrange the debt so that you can make minimum payments. Learn how to do this first so that you do not damage your credit score at the same time. You'll know what amount of payment you can make once you make your Wealth Plan. Remember; you must pay yourself, or invest in yourself, first; every time. You need to start living on less than you earn starting today. By paying yourself the 25% first you ensure that you have 25% to use and help to ensure you live on no more than the 75% that is left over. Most people live on the 75% first and then find out there is no 25% left over. This is the proverbial more month than money syndrome that keeps you living the "Broke-A-Holic" lifestyle.

When you do charge something, have the cash to pay it off in full before an interest payment is due. Many people and businesses would benefit greatly if they used debit cards instead of credit cards. Debit cards have the similar convenience of credit but they do not allow you to live on more than you earn.

Remember the formula: 75/25 = 3. That would be a good place to start your Wealth Planning. Take the debt payment that has the lowest pay off amount and invest all of your investment money in paying off that bill. If you're using the 75/25 = 3 formula that means you will be putting 15% of all your income towards paying that interest bearing debt off. Pay as much as you can, as often as you can, until this debt is eliminated. Once you have eliminated this debt, take all of the money you were paying against it and roll it into the minimum payment you were already making on the next debt with the lowest pay off amount. Do this until all of your interest bearing debts are paid off. Once you've paid off all those debts; credit cards, store cards, payday loans, and others, take that huge amount of money you have been paying on debts and start saving in compounding, interest bearing accounts or investing in income producing assets. Now you are earning the compounding interest instead of being kept broke by paying it. I've mentioned this "domino effect" on eliminating your debt twice now. It can work for you but only if you apply it.

Next are just a few things for you to consider as you develop your own Wealth Plan. It is your choice to keep doing what you are doing now or to make changes that will lead to becoming rich and then wealthy. There is a section in the last chapter of this book for you to jot down your own thoughts and ideas for action as they come to you.

Your Credit Score – Low scores usually mean higher interest rates and bad loans. High scores usually mean access to loans at the best rates available. Having a good credit score is a good thing as long as you don't ruin it by using it to obtain more liabilities. Learn how credit scoring works for individuals and businesses.

Credit Cards (including retail store cards and the like) allow you to spend more than you earn. Switch to debit cards or pay your credit card bill in full every month. Learn how this affects your credit rating as you may want to carry a small monthly balance for credit score purposes.

Eating Out too often (breakfast, lunch, and/or dinner). Pack a lunch to work and have a picnic dinner for some fun every now and then.

Automobiles – yours are too big, too new, too often, rolling over payoffs, driving too fast, carrying too much junk in the trunk, not keeping it maintained, not keeping the correct tire pressure, and you just may have more of them than you really need. The same goes for your boat, motorcycle, and other vehicles.

TV – watching too much = not working your own business during this "TV time", higher bills, too many cable or satellite channels. Wasting time that you should be using for more productive things that contribute to your long term goals.

Computers – web surfing time wasters, purchases on line, game playing, internet expense. Use most of this time to work your own business and to financially educate yourself.

Electronic Gadgets – too many, too often, and too many add-ons (phones, cameras, video cameras, games), watches, GPS's, Flat Screen TV, computer monitors, DVD players, in-home theaters, stereo systems (home & car), DVD players in your car, PDA, PDA/Phone plans that you pay more for in "for use" charges like text messages and data downloads.

Alcohol – Putting your money down the drain.

Tobacco – Your money going up in smoke.

Vacations that you charge and can't pay off in full at the end of the billing period.

Wasting Electricity (electronics, LED lights, no solar, power left on, lights left on, etc).

Wasting Water (sinks, toilets, grass, car washing, laundry, etc).

Not Recycling – that's literally throwing money away to say nothing of the negative environmental effects.

Music CD purchases (store, shipping clubs), buy on-line downloads and only pay for the songs you want.

DVD movie purchases (store, shipping clubs). Use rental services with no late charges or download on your PDA or iPOD. Check out from the library.

Movies at the Theater (popcorn, soda, nachos, candy, etc is where they really get you). Watch the matinee instead of "prime time."

Coffee – Look how much these cost you now; wow!

Soda – These cost a lot if you buy from a vending machine. Almost any purchase from a vending machine is too expensive. How much are you spending at vending machines every day or week?

Cell Phone Plans (too much on it you don't use or not enough for what you do use – minutes, texting, data). Sometimes "unlimited" is cheaper – know your usage patterns.

Home phone plan (too much for not enough – do you even use your home phone anymore?).

ATM Fees – stop paying them; see the teller.

Bank Fees – negotiate to stop paying them or get them reduced. When you have a large account they tend to be more receptive to your requests to lower or eliminate these fees and charges.

Late Payment Fees – pay on time and save money. Automate your payments if you have to so you avoid these money eating fees.

Driving (consolidate trips, carpool, stop fast starts, speeding and associated tickets, cost of gas, etc).

Employee (only paid enough to not quit, pay taxes then live, then nothing left to save).
- o Business Owner (paid as much as possible, pay expenses then pay taxes, own nothing but control everything is the way to go).

Designer clothing, shoes, and accessories – do you really need all of them? There are plenty of quality clothes available at reasonable prices.

Holiday Shopping on credit. Buy gifts before "the season", on sale, pay cash, mail early.

Gambling (includes lottery tickets).

Newspaper subscriptions – read at library.

Magazine subscriptions – read at library.

Pets (Pets are fine – realize most are liabilities).

Someone else manages your: stocks, mutual fund, IRA, 401K and you pay them to do it. Why not manage your own and not pay them to advise you on higher commission purchases. Learn about self-directed IRAs.

Shopping without a list.

Not using coupons.

No emergency cash reserve so you have to charge that unexpected repair or purchase.

No Wealth Plan (budget).

No financial goal.
- o   Debt Free = Getting back to Zero.
- o   Have a better goal than Zero.

Medical Expenses (medicine costs, doctor visit costs – not in shape, not active, overweight, bad food, stress, no relaxation = sick).

No charitable donations (tithing, charity = tax write offs).

No action = No change.

Too big a house & all those mortgage fees.

Renting everything: no equity position, no appreciation, no tax benefits. Sometimes renting is better – instead of a vacation home for once a year use, rent a suite for that week and save a lot of money over the rest of the year.

You're single (no tax benefits).

You're married (no plan, no budget, no control, no goal, no conversation).

You pay your bills BEFORE you pay yourself and then there is never any money left for investments in yourself and your financial future.

No personal financial or business reading or development.

You don't pay your kids a salary for expenses, education, medical, retirement plan. Get them on your own business payroll and use their pay to buy what they need and want. This is maximizing tax laws to your benefit. Have an accountant.

You don't have an accountant to help you maximize the tax laws to your benefit.

Get it now attitude rather than wait to afford it.

Stamps – save money, pay bills on-line (auto pay = no stamps & never late fee. Also frees up your time).

Doing it all yourself. Pay someone $20/hour to do your bills twice a month for two hours each time. Pay someone $10/hour to run your errands once a week for three hours. This assumes you will do something with the time you saved that will generate more income than cash you paid out. More TV or computer game time isn't the goal for this one.

Gym membership that you don't use. (You could make this a business expense – more on that later.)

Book club membership for books you don't read.

Tie club membership and now you have 100 different ties that you don't wear.

Using Home Equity loans to pay off installment debts then charging those debts up again AND now having the equity loan to pay back also.

Excessive amounts of clothing & shoes.

Student Loans (work while in school and graduate with no loan payment or use the money you invested starting at age 3 by putting away $15 dollars a month into a compounding, interest bearing account).

Sports tickets that aren't business deductions.

You believe you will be broke. You must work hard for money mentality. Money is hard to get – scarcity mentality. Wealthy people work less hard than most but make more. Most hard workers are or end up broke.

Belief that money is evil. Rich people are evil. Poverty must be best. Money neither makes you good or evil. Money just gives you more options and makes you more of what you already are.

Listening to your family & friends (they're broke too) tell you it will never work and you can't do it.

This list of considerations is not all inclusive. You will find other items that you want to consider as you develop your plan to become rich or wealthy. They are all your choices. Just make informed decisions about how you handle each of them and the others that you identify throughout your life and the life of your business. Things will change and your plan will need to change with them. If, for example, you decide to stop drinking coffee to save that money for investing you might do that for the next three years. But then, in three years, after acquiring numerous assets you find that you can again drink coffee everyday because of the cash flow you receive from those assets, then by all means, get the coffee. Maybe you decide you like coffee and want to keep drinking it. Fine, reduce the amount each day or week and cut back on the smoking to get you living on less than you earn. Not only will stopping smoking save you money by not buying the smokes, it will most likely save you money on health expenses and possibly insurance costs.

The way you decide to achieve your riches or wealth and put an end to your "Broke-A-Holic" lifestyle has to fit your goals and objectives. This is a personal, family, or business mix and match solution that you will develop. You are designing your own Wealth Plan that will get you to your financial goals.

Wealth Path! You're on it or you're not. Get On It!

Some of What You Don't Know

What you don't know is probably costing you a lot of money. This is why you must educate yourself about money and business. You must become financially literate. The question you must ask yourself is, "*What is the cost of NOT being financially educated*?" This book should not the end of your learning but rather the beginning or continuation of your learning. Following the 75/25 = 3 formula and principles are the only things you will ever need to know and do to get you on your Wealth Path but this chapter will get you thinking, and hopefully acting, on some of the most important concepts of how to become rich or wealthy. This chapter outlines a few of the many things you should know and be doing that you probably don't know and are keeping you from becoming rich or wealthy. These things will also steal your riches and wealth from you once you have them if you do not know about them and how they generate income or expenses as assets or liabilities for you.

Statistically speaking, as I understand, most people who win lotteries or come into other windfalls of money typically are back to their normal income and lifestyle within about five years. That is because they did not know how or what to do with the riches or wealth they had obtained.   Statistically speaking, about only 1% of Americans will retire wealthy at age 65. Approximately 4% of Americans will retire financially independent at age 65. Now that may sound good but realize when we say financially independent the U.S. government defines that as earning just around $36,000, or more, per year. That means only around 5% of Americans earn more than $36,000 per year in retirement according to the statistics I've seen. I don't think most of us would consider $36,000 a year in America during retirement as financially independent nor would it allow you to truly be retired.

Is that what all your hard work and sacrifice is leading you to? Is this what you said when you graduated from high school, "Hey, I want to work for the next 45 years, spending 40 or more hours a week doing work related stuff, maybe taking a week vacation each year, but having to check voicemail and email even while on vacation, miss most of my children's and family activities because of 'critically important' work that has to been done right now, every day, just to end up maybe in the top 5% of retired Americans, earning $36,000 a year in retirement?" Oh yeah, that's the dream isn't it? Living the 75/25 = 3 lifestyle may not help you cut back on work hours but it sure will help you on your walk along the Wealth Path to retiring within the top 1% of American's.

As we are tending to live longer and expenses are increasing we find our working years extending as well because we cannot afford to retire, or live, if we stop working at age 65. There is nothing wrong with working beyond age 65, if you want to. The problem is the millions of people who work beyond age 65 because they have to. Statistically speaking, at least in America, we're collectively doing something wrong if so many people simply cannot afford to stop working. Statistically speaking, it's because we are not getting a financial education and what we don't know is keeping us living the "Broke-A-Holic" lifestyle.

There are many other resources available you can learn from that will teach you more about what you don't know you don't know financially that are probably costing you money and stealing from you financial future right now. There are also many other resources about how owning your own small business can help you become rich or wealthy while maximizing tax laws, to your benefit, for you and your family. For those who've stuck with the book this far you can ask me about some resources I recommend for becoming financially educated, learning about starting and running your own business, and for resource help with things that affect your money like taxes and accounting to help you find ways to keep, grow, and use the riches and wealth you generate from following the 2 Steps for riches and wealth. Send an email to contact@wealthpathbook.com with this subject line: "I Must Get Financially Educated". You will get a reply with my recommendations. If you don't think you need to email me about this read the rest of this chapter.

As one example of what you don't know that you don't know, and it's probably costing you money, let's look briefly at why you should own your own business. When you own your own business tax laws tend to treat you better as a business owner. Owning your own business can be an asset for you by putting money in your pocket not only from your business profits but also from your legal tax strategies. Yes, that's right, as a business owner paying taxes can be something to look forward to.

The #1 Tax Strategy for Americans is to Start Your Own Small Business. Keep your full time job for now but from a tax perspective owning your own business gives your accountant something to work with. This also gives you something to fall back on if you're laid off. You should start your own business now so it is up and running before you find out you are getting laid off. When you do start your own business remember that good records are critical. Start-up costs, including education and training for that business, can be written off the next year once your business makes at least $1.00 in profit.

You can start your business as a Sole Proprietorship (the worst for doing business, but better than not doing a business, as this way offers you no legal protection), an LLC, an S-Corp, a C-Corp, a Joint Venture or Partnership, or one of a several other business entities. The key is to learn which entity best fits the business you will own. Some considerations for selecting the business structure you will need to set up are:

1.   What Type of Income are You Creating
2.   Your Asset Protection needs
3.   Where are You doing Business
4.   Partnership Considerations
5.   Administrative Issues

If you decide to make your LLC from a $35.00 online website you will have a $35.00 LLC that you might not need and that might not maximize your tax strategies for the business you have. Is that what you really want as a business owner? Probably not. Get educated now about setting up the right kind of business entity for you and your business and then get professional help setting up your business as soon as possible. If you think you can't afford to do that, you don't realize just how much it is costing you every year to not have your own business.

As a business owner you can legally pay business expenses before paying taxes. As a W-2 employee your tax deduction opportunities are very limited and your taxes are taken out for you. As a business owner you have the opportunity to take hundreds of deductions. Some of these could be your home, your car, your travel, your phone, your cell phone, your entertainment, your equipment, your supplies, your books, your seminars, your accounting fees, your legal fees, your start up costs, insurance, marketing, employee benefits, retirement plans and contributions, office expenses, utilities, banking expenses, internet services, your gym membership, or portions of all the above, and much, much more. Always ask yourself, and your accountant, as a business owner, "How can I legally make what I am doing tax deductible?" and then do it. "How can I maximize my business tax strategies to legally keep or control more of what I earn?" and then do it.

Go ahead; take a look at IRS Publications 535 and 463 to see for yourself if you pay taxes in the United States. Then go interview an accountant or tax attorney or a couple of them. Make a list of business and tax questions, call and tell them you are going to start your own business, ask them for a free hour consultation at their office for you to interview them and see if they are the right fit for your business, and then go interview them. Ask all the "dumb" questions you can think of about how starting and owning your own business can make much of your life tax deductible and keep more of your money in your pocket, working for you every day. Take notes on everything they tell you. I prefer real estate as my business because it is everywhere, it offers so many tax strategy options, and in one good deal I can make more income than most Americans earn in an entire year of work. You can decide on any business you want. Maybe your business will be Avon, ACN, Mona Vie, Pre-Paid Legal, Amway, a day care center, a pet walking or sitting service, a house cleaning service, a consulting service, a vending machine business, a used book store, an eBay store, a photography service, a travel planning service, a clothing line, a franchise, a sports bar, or any number of other possibilities that interest you.

Know what business you are going to start when interviewing the accountants and tax attorneys because that will help you ask specific questions and it will help them answer with specifics. You may find out there are better businesses out there you can start than the one you were first thinking about. One of your interview questions could be, "Based on your experience, what small business is the easiest to start up and at the same time, easiest for you to conservatively claim as many deductions as possible?"

When done interviewing all of them pick the best accountant or tax attorney for your business needs and hire them on an "as needed" basis. Paying for their services as you need them is a before taxes business expense by the way. You are now getting professional advice and work done for you with pre-tax dollars that will maximize your rich or wealthy bottom line.

If you spend $600.00 on a professional accountant who does your business taxes, which is a business expense, to get you a $6,000 tax savings, that accountant and his $600.00 fee were assets to you because they put money in your pocket. You also probably save a lot of time by paying that $600.00 that you are then able to devote to your business, thus generating even more income from your business.

The #1 tax strategy for Americans, or those people living in America, is to Start Your Own Small Business. No wonder the wealthy own businesses. Now you should too.

That leads to another point about becoming wealthy. Remember, this book defines wealth as not having to work to generate income. Wealth is having passive income that covers all your expenses and leaves you with enough money left over to be comfortable. So, eventually, as you become rich and begin the transition to wealthy, you are going to hire people to work for you. Hiring people is a good thing. It helps them pay their bills. It helps you make more money while working less or differently. Hiring people is what allows you to have passive income while work is still being done. Hiring people is a pre-tax business expense that allows you to put their time and expertise to work earning you more money than you pay them, generating you wealth.

This is why a highly paid brain surgeon might be rich but not wealthy. A brain surgeon must be there to do the work himself. Eventually he or she runs out of hours they can work in a day. Once they stop working the money from brain surgery stops coming in. For a brain surgeon, or any other highly paid professional, to become wealthy, they must find ways to invest their earned income that will generate passive income for them. A great way to do this is to have a business that allows them to generate income from other people's work. In Timothy Ferriss' popular 2007 book, <u>The 4-Hour Workweek</u>, you can find several ideas about outsourcing work that can help you get on your Wealth Path right now.

What you don't know is probably costing you and your family a lot of money every year. How much is it costing you year after year after year to not be financially educated where you live and work? How much is it costing you to not start, own, and operate your own business? How much is it costing you not to have experts working for you?

If owning your own business could allow you to legally deduct so much of your life expenses when you file taxes, to the point where you could possibly end up legally paying no taxes, despite making a profit, why don't you own your own business right now? The size of your business does not matter. The location of your business does not matter. The time you spend working at your business does not matter. Why don't you own your own business right now and have it employ all of your family members so you can take advantage of every legal tax break offered?

If you could legally generate $1,000 to $10,000 or more in tax deductions because you owned your own business and you could spend that money you saved on taxes doing something you wanted to do instead of paying it in taxes, why don't you own your own business right now? Maybe it's because you didn't know. Maybe it's because you thought it would be too hard. Maybe it's because you think there is nothing you can do as a business. Maybe it's because, just like you, statistically speaking, only about 5% of Americans end up retiring financially independent or wealthy. Maybe it's because you spend all your working hours working as a W-2 employee for someone else who owns a business and takes advantages of all the tax laws that business owners get. Most people work long and hard at their jobs just to stay broke. Wealthy people work differently to stay wealthy, because they are financially educated, and one way they stay wealthy is to own a business or businesses.

There is nothing wrong with having a job. Jobs are important; that's how work gets done and that's how people survive and pay bills. I'm not saying go out and quit your job and open a scarf knitting business tomorrow. I'm saying, keep your job and legitimately open your scarf knitting business today. Keep your job until you are making enough at your scarf knitting business that you can afford to quit your job. Before quitting your job for your new business you had better have cash set aside for the times your scarf knitting business isn't doing so well, like during the summer maybe. I recommend you have at least six months of all your expenses set aside for use when you finally make that decision to quit your job and work your own business full time. You may never quit your job and that is fine also. Just learn about, apply, and take advantage of all the legal tax breaks you get for owning your own business, part-time, on the side.

As another example of what you don't know that you don't know, and it's probably costing you money, let's look briefly at Self-Directed Retirement Plans, or SDRPs. This should get you doing more research on this topic and talking to your current IRA manager, an accountant, perhaps an attorney, and definitely looking up the U.S. Internal Revenue Service information. If you're serious about creating, growing, and keeping wealth, you need to get educated on, understand, and use Self-Directed Retirement Plans (SDRP). Here's why:

- A passive IRA custodian will allow you to self direct your IRA.

- You can combine multiple people's SDRP IRAs to invest in Real Estate (or other investments allowed by law). Not all the investment money has to come from you.

- A retirement plan (RP) is a Trust not an investment. A retirement plan is a vehicle into which you put investments. Your retirement plan becomes the owner of the investments.

- You cannot take profits from a self-directed IRA investment personally unless you actually retire. Otherwise, to get at the profit you would have to partner with your IRA to get a percentage of the profit out. (This is a huge wealth building strategy that you can't afford to miss. If you don't understand what it means you need to become financially literate and get business educated. See the next bullet for an example.)

- Use a Buy Direction Letter to your SDRP to buy shares in an LLC. This can be an LLC you control by the way. This can be an LLC that employs your spouse and children. The LLC has a checkbook. Use the LLC's checkbook to pay for investments, and purchases and you don't have to keep doing Buy Direction Letters over and over. This is called Checkbook Control and you are now making use of your retirement plan money right now, today, with no early withdrawal penalties, etc, to grow your wealth. Get financially educated. Get professional advisors working for you. Get on the Wealth Path.

- A retirement plan is a great tax shelter.

- You can have as many Retirement Plans as you want and at the same time – so can your children if you know how to set that up.

- Defined Contribution Plans (DC Plans) define the contributions (This is how much you can put in annually, etc.).
  - Predetermined fixed amount.
  - Percentage of income.

- Defined Benefit Plans (DB Plans) define the benefits (This is how much you can take out).
  - When you will retire.
  - Up to 50% to 100% of the Grantors highest salary of 5-10 yrs is typical to determine the benefit.
  - How much the Grantor earns.
  - The amount that will be paid to the Grantor during retirement.
  - How long the Grantor will live.
  - The maximum contribution amount for a DB plan can change from year to year.

- Some retirement plans allow a "catch up" provision (pay more in) if you are over 50.

- Lump Sum Distribution Option instead of the Annuity (yearly distribution).
  - Once you choose the annuity you CAN NOT go back and choose lump sum later.

- You must have earned income (W2 or 1099 DIV) to contribute to a Retirement Plan – but you can continue to put money into the plan that is earned by investments the plan has made. This is another huge wealth building strategy you can use. If you don't understand it you need to get financially literate and business educated.

- If you are a W-2 employee contributing the minimum required amount into your company retirement plan to get 100% of your employer's matching funds is another wealth building strategy. These matching funds are free wealth building money for you. Put all the rest of your retirement contribution money into your own SDRP.

- Section 408 of IRS Code & IRS Publication 590 define what your RP can invest in.

- In a SDRP Passive Custodians take possession of your RPs. Passive Custodians will not sell you investments, give you advice, or pressure you to buy anything. They will track and document your transactions without trying to sell you on buying "company pushed" investments.

- You can purchase or inherit someone else's IRA. If it has matured, you can receive the benefits tax free.

- When passed on to beneficiaries the RP becomes a Beneficial RP. If money comes out of the plan at this time it is taxable money. You can pass it on tax free or tax deferred and not count against inheritance taxes and avoid probate. It is better for a person to inherit an RP than for a trust to inherit it. A trust will have to pay taxes. If the RP is already in a trust then ensure or change it to a "See Through" provision so the benefits pass directly to a person as the beneficiary. Make sure you consult an Estate Planner to set this up correctly and keep a copy of the Beneficial Forms so they are not "lost". This is another huge piece of wealth information if you want to pass on your accumulated riches or wealth. Get financially educated.

- Two types of 401k Rollovers:
    - Direct Rollover (no taxes withheld). This is a good thing but many people do not set up their rollover correctly and end up doing a 60-Day Rollover because they don't know any better.
    - 60-Day Rollover or Indirect Rollover (taxes withheld at 20% less than you get with a Direct Rollover) You must return 100% of the amount taken out into the new plan even though they withheld 20% when they "gave you your check".

- Retirement Plans cannot purchase:
    - Life insurance in your name.

- o S-Corporations.
- o Collectables.
- o Cars, Art, Metals & Gems, Rugs & Antiques, Alcohol, Stamps & Coins (can purchase any investment allowed by law).

- Do all your SDRP investing with attorney and CPA advice and counsel.

- Two Good Taxes your SDRP can pay:
  - o Unrelated Business Taxable Income (UBTI). – when you get income, like rents

  - o Unrelated Debt Financed Income (UDFI). – when you leverage your RP, like it's purchase potential with a non-recourse loan (they can take the property but can't affect your credit score) like a hard money loan – the percentage financed will create taxable profits at that same percentage.

- Self-Directed Retirement Plans can give business loans. The loans are paid back, with interest at rates you set, into your SDRP retirement plan. You have to use a RP that has a loan provision in it so put that provision in your SDRP. Again, use a professional Passive Custodian and attorney to set this up right. You could then use this provision in your SDRP to make short term loans to real estate or other investors or businesses right now. Your SDRP becomes "THE BANK". The payments and interest go back into your SDRP when they repay you. If they don't repay you and your loan was to a real estate investor your SDRP gets the property. Either way, you build your wealth right now using retirement plan money that everyone else thinks they can't touch for many years to come. No wonder the wealthy are wealthy. Become financially literate and business educated.

Ask your current retirement plan coordinator or custodian or your current broker about these Self-Directed Retirement Plans. First, they may not even know what they are. Second, they will probably tell you that they are illegal or you can't do one. They are however, legal, and you can do one. In fact, you can do as many as you like. Check the IRS Code, Section 408. Read IRS Publication 590. Self-Directed Retirement Accounts are just one way you could dramatically be increasing your riches or wealth but you probably have never heard of them.

Your current retirement plan may not allow you to self-direct your plan and it may significantly restrict what you can invest in but that is because it is written into that plan that the plan will only purchase specific things. So, if you signed up for that plan of course you will be restricted and not allowed to self-direct your plan. That does not mean Self-Directed Retirement Plans are illegal. It just means you are probably not maximizing the benefits and potential growth and investment options you could have if you did have a Self-Directed Retirement Plan.

Once you do find out about Self-Directed Retirement Plans you'll probably be told it costs too much to set them up or you'll have to pay penalties during the transfer. Not if you do it right. Get yourself financially educated. Your Self-Directed Retirement Plan could be a huge asset in generating riches and wealth but only if you know how and only if you do it. As with taxes, setting up companies and businesses, and other investments, get professional advice about Self-Directed Retirement Plans. You've got the IRS information about them now so don't let anyone tell you they are illegal or don't exist. Follow the rules, play the money-making game, and use this information to start transforming your financial life. You can change your financial future right now. You can start that change by doing something like setting up and using a SDRP to start acquiring income producing assets. The benefits can be huge. By learning just about Self-Directed Retirement Plans in this book you have more than earned back the money you spent for this book but only if you take educated, informed, and advised action. Thinking about it and then not taking action will mean that you have continued to do your routine things routinely and your future remains unchanged.

One more thing that you didn't know you didn't know is that you can retire at anytime in America. You don't have to wait until you are 59 or 65 or 72 to retire. You can retire at 25 or 30 or 45 or any other age. Get yourself financially educated. Learn about a 72T early retirement distribution and how you can retire at any age without withdrawal penalties from your retirement accounts. That's all I'm going to say about it.

Another thing you probably don't know you didn't know; you can employ your spouse, children, friends, and anyone else you want in your own business and give all your employees benefits you want like education benefits, health benefits, retirement plan matching funds, and more all using before tax dollars. This is another reason that starting your own business is a key to becoming wealthy.

The great thing about being able to employ your children is you can pay them an income and set up their own retirement plans at any age. Instead of buying their clothes, toys, school supplies, movie tickets, iPods, cell phones, video games, and paying for their college tuition using your own, after tax dollars, you can now use the money they earn to pay for those things and more while using your business before tax dollars to pay them their salary. Best of all, this is already set up so that your children legally pay no taxes on up to a certain amount of money they earn. As of this book writing that is $5,700.00 per year. Of course, we have not even mentioned the gift tax exclusion. Get financially educated.

Wouldn't life be better if you could use that kind of money every year, pre-tax dollars, to buy your children the things you're buying them now using your own after-tax dollars? That amount is per child who is employed, by the way. You can do this for your children at any age, starting at newborn. Imagine hiring and employing your newborn baby and legitimately paying him or her $5,700.00, or whatever the current, legal amount is, in the first year of life and every year of life thereafter, for the next 18 years. All the while your child legally pays no taxes and has a self-directed retirement plan making investments and earning additional income from those investments (like rental properties) for those same 18 years. Now drop in some gift money to those accounts every year as well.

What could your child's financial status look like in 18 years? What could yours look like in 18 years for that matter? What could be different for you and your children if they had $100,000 in investments, earning additional passive income each month, at the age of 18? Couple that with a financial education for them along the way and your child could perhaps retire wealthy at age 25 after "working" only the first 25 years of their life because, as you researched under a 72T early retirement distribution, you can retire at any age in America. Would this change your financial future and that of your children? I think it would. What is it costing you to *NOT* be financially educated? We've only touched the surface of things you don't know that you don't know and that are probably costing you a lot of money every year. That means it is costing you your financial future right now. That is why only 5% of Americans retire financially independent or wealthy.

For those of you living outside of the United States find out about the financial and money making rules where you live and work. Regardless of what country you live in you have to become financially educated and learn the rules of generating riches and wealth by those rules, in that country, while living the 2 laws of riches and wealth.

Of course you also probably don't know anything about estate planning and how that can be a significant benefit or loss to you financially. When estate planning is tied into many of these other business and financial strategies it can complete or it can destroy your riches or wealth. This book is not about estate planning but if you want your riches or wealth to keep working and to maximize tax and legal strategies you had better get educated on estate planning and you had better get yourself a competent estate planner who can tie all of your other business and personal assets and strategies together into an estate plan that does what you want it to do. It is never too early to start putting together an estate plan. These are not just for the rich and wealthy, they are for everyone. Start your estate planning right now by preparing a will. By having a will you have taken the first step in making your estate plan. Of course, your will is no good if nobody knows about it and nobody can find it so once you make it let someone know about it and where it is stored.

What you don't know is probably costing you and your children a lot of money. This is why you must educate yourself and become financially and business ownership literate. You must help your children become financially and business ownership literate as well. Getting a good education should also include getting educated about money, finances, business ownership, wealth, and asset protection. If we include that curriculum in our "get a good education" advice perhaps, statistically speaking, more of us will be able to actually retire wealthy at age 65 than currently do.

That email address is contact@wealthpathbook.com and the subject line is, "I Must Get Financially Educated" if you want my recommendations on where to start getting this financial and business education. You should decide to take action and send that email right now. This book is about the 2 Steps, or laws, of becoming rich or wealthy but you must know that there is a lot out there that will help you live the 2 Steps of becoming rich or wealthy.

How much is it costing you right now to <u>not</u> be financially literate and business educated? Get educated and get on the Wealth Path!

Conclusion

That's it. One step to rich and one more step to wealthy. There's nothing hard about the two steps. They are universally applicable. It does not matter what language you speak, what country you live in, or what religion you believe. It does not matter what your level of education is but it does matter what your education is about. It does not matter what job or business you have. If you have an income and apply the principles outlined in this book you can become rich or wealthy.

Live on 75% or less of the income you earn. Give 10% of your income to charitable sources. Invest 15% of your income in compounding, interest bearing accounts, consistently, over time or in purchasing ever increasing income producing assets. Stop paying compounding interest and start collecting compounding interest. If you can't make these percentages right now apply the principles outlined and do what you can starting today until you can live the 75/25 = 3 formula.

The time to start living this way is right now. Just decide to do it and then do it. Write down your Wealth Plan and your financial goals, look at them every day, and then surpass your financial goals. If you have a spouse, children, siblings, parents, friends, or associates share this information with them so they also begin the journey to financial literacy and wealth that you are now on. If you know someone in high school or college they need this book right now, today, over-night expressed to them. Order it and ship it to them right now. Help all these people change their financial future.

It's not how much you make that matters, it's how much you keep for investing while living or running your business below your means that matters. It's what you know and how you choose to take action or not.

If you earn $200.00 an hour but live a lifestyle that spends $300.00 an hour you are broke. If you earn $12.00 an hour but live a lifestyle that spends only $9.00 an hour you are set to become rich or wealthy.

Become financially literate and business educated, start your own legitimate business, get professional advice, become rich or wealthy. You choose every day to be a financial victim or a financial victor. Do something. The choice is yours. You now have the knowledge to start changing your future right now but for that to happen you must decide to take action every day.

Wealth Path. Get On It! or not. You decide daily.

Your Actions

- _____
- _____
- _____
- _____
- _____
- _____
- _____
- _____
- _____
- _____
- _____
- _____

- _____
- _____
- _____
- _____
- _____
- _____
- _____
- _____
- _____
- _____
- _____
- _____
- _____
- _____

- _____

- _____

- _____

- _____

- _____

- _____

- _____

- _____

- _____

- _____

- _____

- _____

- _____

- _____

- _____
- _____
- _____
- _____
- _____
- _____
- _____
- _____
- _____
- _____
- _____
- _____
- _____
- _____

Additional Reading List
(in no particular order)

Rich Dad Poor Dad by Robert Kiyosaki

Creating Wealth by Robert G. Allen

Make Your Life Tax Deductible by David W. Meier

Get Rich, Stay Rich, Pass It On by Catherine S. McBreen and George H. Walper, Jr.

The 4-Hour Work Week by Timothy Ferris

Credit Revolution: Path of the Smart Consumer by John C. Heath, Esq., Dr. Randy Padwer, and Jayson R. Orvis

Emerging Real Estate Markets by Dave Lindahl

Multi-Family Millions by Dave Lindahl

Short-Sale Pre-Foreclosure Investing by Dwan Bent-Twyford and Sharon Restrepo

Lawyers are Liars by Mark J. Kohler, Attorney & CPA